Adventure into Your Destiny
Copyright © 2006 by H. Robert Stoppard
Destiny Unlimited International
406 West Lexington Road, Lititz, PA 17543
(717) 627-0480   www.destinyui.com

All rights reserved.

ISBN 10: 0-9778614-2-2
ISBN 13: 978-0-9778614-2-2

Partnership Publications
A Division of House to House Publications
www.H2HP.com

Unless otherwise noted, all scripture quotations in this publication are taken from the
Holy Bible, New International Version (NIV). © 1973, 1978, 1984 by International
Bible Society. Used by permission of Zondervan Publishing House. All rights reserved.

Printed in the United States of America
Cover and layout design: Nancy Stawitz

Adventure into Your Destiny

A Life Journal

H. Robert Stoppard

Partnership
Publications

A Division of House to House Publications

"A journey of a thousand miles
begins
with a
single step."
—Confucius

Acknowledgments

The journey to the discovery of life in its fullness has been hidden in a series of mysteries that can only be explained by the One who created us. I give credit to God for the wisdom and direction to piece together a purposeful life that often seemed impossible to amount to anything.

A special "thank you" goes out to all who believed in me and my family as we changed careers in 1998. The testimonies of your lives have provided many of the insights we use to create the many dynamic resources we offer at Destiny Unlimited International which includes this journal.

I saved the most special thanks for last. My wife, Ann, along with my sons, Joshua and Matthew, have endured many ventures in to the wilderness areas of life as I continued to risk and try new things. Ann's challenging questions and innate desire for truth kept me digging deep to find practical answers to some of life's questions. My family's belief in me during the difficult times as well as the good inspired me to continue onward in the adventure of my own destiny.

Contents

"Make a careful exploration
of who you are and the
work you have been given,
and then sink yourself into that.
Don't be impressed with yourself.
Don't compare yourself with
others. Each of you must take
responsibility for doing the
creative best you can with
your own life."

—Paul of Tarsus
Galatians 6:4-5 (Message)

Introduction

Every person has a vital role to play in the world. You may not know it, but deep within you is a unique design that will never match any other individual on the earth. Yes, there will be others who will have similar preferences, careers, social status and the like; however, your own presentation will be like none other. As we take this journey together it will be of utmost importance that you are relaxed and that you have minimal distractions. Some quiet music in the background may help you relax, but that is a personal preference. Dedicating specified time frames to be still, and to listen and write, will greatly improve your success; however, you will also encounter moments when you feel a sporadic urge to write. When this happens, do so without delay, even if it is in the middle of the night.

Mankind is designed to work together, each specializing in various aspects of life. Because of this design we find ourselves needing one another to each prosper fully. There is a powerful advancement that comes when two or more people annex their abilities, strengths and ideas. Think of a building crew, for example. One carpenter will be able to build two complete house walls in a day's time. However, if you team three carpenters together, suddenly you can frame an entire first floor of a house and more, each one having varying degrees of experience and each having different strengths, but unified to accomplish the goal.

I know you might be thinking, "But you don't know me, I have not accomplished much of anything since I was born!"

It is not about what you have accomplished, or even about how much money you have made. True success is not a position or an accumulation of "stuff," but a sense of self-worth, fulfillment and value from making a positive impact on the lives of others. It is only from this platform that you will engage a life of purpose. Some have become very wealthy, but at whose expense? What kind of trail have they left behind them? In what condition are their relationships—even their health? **When a person can settle into a place of internal value, life will begin to take a positive and fruitful direction.**

Sadly, many spend a lot of energy trying to overcompensate for the parts of their belief system that do not promote life. If you want to find rest, you must find purpose. Don't get me wrong: I am not saying life is never wearisome. Hard work tires a mind and body. I am saying that when a balance is established in your entire being, rest will be a by-product of the peace you experience. Both mentally and emotionally, you will find a synergy that promotes creativity and allows for spontaneous decision-making. Peace, in the fullness of its meaning, is not an absence of trouble, but a tranquil state of being in the midst of trouble. This does not mean you will never feel fear. The important thing is not to "be afraid" and be caught up in the trouble. The essence of the type of peace I am talking about is consequential of an intimate walk with God.

An Overview

Each day of a person's life is like a page in a book. Of course we cannot remember everything, but it is important to know that key attributes of your life can be discovered as you begin to write what comes to mind naturally. We will spend time looking at your past, your present and your future. The pages you write will amaze you and those with whom you share. You will discover just how important your past is when you take a careful look at your future. Each section of your new life journal will help you understand the value of each stage, as well as giving you important leads to extracting your creativity and highlighting the unique facets of your own person.

Part 1 is entitled, "Redeeming the Past." This section is designed to help process life's hurts, as well as quicken your spirit to recognize the hidden dreams, desires and life-giving experiences that are vital to your future. As you write the pages of your past, you will find clues to your future, hence the paradox that your past is an important part of your future!

Part 2 is entitled, "Balancing Your Present." You will discover the wholeness of prosperity and how it impacts your life. When life is out of balance in certain areas, our whole being is impacted because we need to live in a state of equilibrium. As you write, you will find yourself discovering practical solutions for bringing that much needed peace into your present circumstances, freeing you to dream about your future.

Part 3 is entitled, "Inspiring Hope for Your Future." Human life was designed in the image of God. He, in His infinite wisdom, has stored up mysteries for each individual to discover, unlock and effectuate during his or her lifetime. Many have lost their ability to dream, and sadly, have let their good desires fade away into a hidden place of their being. There is good news: you will discover that nothing is lost. The wise and caring God who created the heavens and earth gave us a promise which many do not claim or seek; He said, "I will cause all things to work out for good for those who love Him." This means that the hurtful, and even terrible, things that happened in our past can be transformed somehow for good, later in life; it does not mean that the terrible or hurtful thing that happened was good. As you continue writing your book, you will find passion for life emerging, and inspiration springing forth. You will find the courage to risk again and inspire others to do the same.

You have a vital role to play!

Who you are is important, no matter what others around you have said when you were growing up. What I have found is that hurting people hurt people. However, the inverse is also true; people alive in their destinies inspire others to do the same. People with limited, or no purpose, tend to blame-shift, hence tempting those around them to live similarly. **If you want lasting change that leads you into a life of success, your time has come!**

"In life
what sometimes
appears to be
the end is
really a new
beginning."
—Author Unkown

1 Redeeming the Past

Your past is an important part of your future! Life experience contains valuable gems that greatly impact your ability to walk in the fullness of your destiny. Have you ever considered that critical keys to your future may be waiting in the chronicles of your history for discovery? You may say, "You just don't know how bad I've had it! I've failed at so many things. Besides, you just don't know how poorly I have been treated!" Many are simply on hold, waiting for their supernatural call to destiny and purpose, but are losing the hope that their life will ever matter. If this is you, consider the possibility that your destiny has been, and continues to, unfold without your realization. As we continue this study together there is an important thought to consider: "*Embracing the entirety of your life produces the*

15

greatest value." **The only loss is what you consider to be lost.** There is no way you can truly consider where you are going if you do not honestly evaluate where you are, and your life to the present day.

Sadly, many people continue to be controlled by the past, trapped in fears and disappointments. When this happens, **fear overtakes your life and manages it for you.** The prevalence of fear as the controlling factor in so many lives is ironic, since most of what people fear never actually happens. Additionally, many suffer from low energy and spend an astounding 65-75% of their emotional energy preventing what they fear might happen. Fears are often not conscious thoughts, but are underlying, hidden urges that prompt our decisions. This state is incredibly frustrating and can cause us to spend most of our lives in "minimal survival mode." The stress of this way of living causes physical, mental and emotional ailments, and **a destiny of managing pain**.

There is good news for those who begin to face these issues. As they begin to own up to the truth of their situation, they will find themselves creating an environment where truth is invited into life. The wonderful thing about truth is that it *sets you free*. The load is lightened, the body can rest, and the shaping of a life-giving destiny begins. Again, you may say, "You don't know how hard I have tried! Nothing seems to work." Denying or forgetting your past—and keeping hidden fears hidden—does not create an environment that fosters truth.

In order to benefit most from this section of your Life Journal, spend some time over the next few weeks writing about your life from conception up to your present age. You can begin by recording comments on your perspective of the family in which you were born. Think about the attributes that were inspiring to you and explain how they positively impacted your life. You will also remember hurtful and negative memories as you write. Processing such events through writing helps bring closure if you are honest about your feelings. Often it will be important to forgive those who brought pain into your life, so as you press on simply write, "I choose to forgive _____ for the hurt, disappointment or abuse they inflicted on my life." It is likely that you may have to ask forgiveness also: "Dear _____, please forgive me for the way I hurt you or wrongfully judged you." These statements can be elaborated upon as you continue to process the pain.

As you continue to look at your life, write on topics like:
· What you once dreamed about
· Things you enjoyed
· Things you disliked or even hated
· Important people in your life
· School friends or school "enemies"
· Favorite teachers and why you liked them so much
· Hobbies or sports you loved to do or wished you could do
· How you got along with your siblings
· Accomplishments that were celebrated
· Unfair circumstances

Were there times you wanted to try things but were held back because of a parent's fears? If so, spend some time writing about how this impacted your life. Speak from your heart about what you would do if you had another chance. These exercises will help you be honest with yourself about your successes and your failures. You will also ignite passion for those "suppressed" desires as you release the pain surrounding them. Make note of such things in the last section of the book so that you can write about them elsewhere in greater detail.

It is not important to get this all done before you move on. The idea of this journal is to write about what is important from your past, what you need to balance in your present and what you want to do with your future. Let yourself be free and go where your heart leads you.

71

"Go confidently in the direction
of your dreams.

Live the life you have imagined."
—Henry David Thoreau

2   Balancing Your Present

For the most part, individuals who are honest with themselves can recognize when they are out of balance in various aspects of their lives. This brings confusion to the mind, will and emotions, as well as the physical body, which is trying to maintain equilibrium. The imbalance is usually derived from lies we believe about life, society and God. Hence, what drives the decisions you are making in your life, which may seem right but are not producing good results, are the beliefs stored in your memory. We often do not know what we believe, but we can touch upon them if we honestly examine the results we are experiencing. If we play the victim we will continually find reasons and excuses for our dysfunction and will need to blame someone or something; or worse: sabotage ourselves by condemning ourselves. Facts can be our friend if we take time to carefully discern what is causing ill circumstances. Generally, the pain and heartache we experience is linked directly to what we believe. Of course, if you suffer some abuse or manipulation, pain will result. When we devote the necessary time to be open and honest with ourselves, we will inevitably find that much of our disappointment comes from our imbalance in life. Accordingly, if you want to find out what you truly believe, set goals for specific changes and you will quickly notice the excuses and reasons that seemingly emerge from nowhere. Make note of those excuses so that you can extirpate and replace them with genuine truth as you uncover your strengths and weaknesses. Remember that weaknesses are not inherently bad attributes. Where you find yourself lacking is a good place to find others who have strengths in those areas, so that they can help balance your journey.

In order to best find success in our present we should evaluate the wholeness of the term "prosperity." Prosperity is a hot topic today—even in the religious world. My discovery is that true prosperity develops when six areas of life are all healthily balanced. To paint a realistic picture of your life in this area, you must be honest and forthright as you examine each aspect and record how you view them. If you are willing to be vulnerable, ask someone else who knows you well to give you insight as to how healthy you are in each area.

Prosperity is six-fold:
- Spiritual
- Mental
- Emotional

- Relational
- Financial
- Physical

Any area in which you are not actively growing or maturing will bring an imbalance to your life, creating stumbling blocks to fulfilling your destiny.

Everything in life requires some type of fuel or energy source with which to produce its end or intended result. Prosperity is no different. Without the proper energy source the only possible result is decay, loss or death.

True prosperity is only possible to those who are *alive in their destiny*. Reflect upon this equation for several minutes, then journal your thoughts: **Your personality, plus your gift mix, plus your gender, plus your family of origin, plus your life experience equals a unique and wonderful person who can succeed.** In other words, your heart can sing, your life has purpose and the mundane details of life even have meaning."

Now, let's focus on the fuel that spurs us into action, pain or passion.

The meaning of passion in the context of our discussion is *boundless enthusiasm*. Passion is often a misunderstood and misdirected force. In a culture that uses sexuality to arouse passion in order to market products, we could easily misunderstand the value of this "boundless enthusiasm." As you come alive in your destiny, passion will ebb and flow according to the stage or season you are experiencing. Waiting for certain aspects of your life purpose to come into alignment is one of those seasons. Another season that can be painful is the process of understanding finances. The lack of money is never the problem. Money is merely the exchange of trust. This comment will need some time to become a revelation, because we are used to looking at what we don't have rather than what is possible. Building solid relationships where another can trust you to carry out your vision will invite finances to match the need.

Passion stays alive:
- When others are included in the dream
- By embracing the bad times as a value
- As you continue to take risks
- When you come to peace with self

As positive results become apparent, your unique design is validated and harnessed to serve a purpose. During this stage an unusual revelation begins to make sense—that the help we often need comes in the form of pain.

There are two types of pain: pain is either a motivator or a prison.

Life-Giving Pain, i.e., disciplines we embrace in order to accomplish our goals
- Something you choose
- Becomes energy
- Builds character
- Produces results
- Inspires integrity
- Defines our strengths

The good news is that life-giving pain does not last very long when chosen freely and handled responsibly.

Life-Stealing Pain = indecision, denial, procrastination, avoidance, blaming others, excuses
- Self-made prison
- Usually blame-shifts
- Drains energy
- Quenches passion
- Breaks relationships
- Never satisfied

Note: Even this pain, if embraced as a value can be turned into Life-giving pain. A simple act of forgiving yourself, admitting your fear, and seeking forgiveness from those who have been negatively impacted, will prepare the way to experience the freedom necessary to move on in your destiny.

How do you get life-giving pain?
- Set goals
- Invest time
- Invest money
- Be held accountable
- Make obtainable choices
- By making mistakes

How do you get or revive passion?
- Dream
- Imagine
- Tell others
- Read about other people's success stories
- Write

Passion is kept alive by setting reasonable goals and experiencing the satisfaction of results.

To best help you discover the fullness of prosperity we have prepared an exercise, "Balancing the Present," located at the end of this section. If you do the exercise now you will soon discover what you need to write about in this section; i.e., you can write about the successes and frustrations you are currently experiencing. Now is the time to write about some short-term goals that will help bring you the peace, rest and equilibrium you so desperately seek. If you want to speed up the process, invite a trusted friend to help hold you accountable to accomplishing your newly defined goals. As you process the challenge, remember to reiterate the aforementioned motivators. Write about how you presently feel, then about how you expect to feel when accomplishing those goals.

"Adversity is
the state in which
man most easily
becomes acquainted
with himself, being especially
free of admirers then."

—John Wooden

Prosperity Worksheet

Rate the qualities of each attribute on the following scale: 0 - need a lot of improvement, up to 10 - doing very well. Each of the following attributes will give you clues as to what needs balance as you continue your journey. As you rate them take special note of the areas you want to grow in and find balance. We have found that any category that is off balance adds stress to the rest of your life. A word of caution, this worksheet is to help you grow, not cause you to be self-condemning. Therefore, celebrate where you are finding success and then set small goals to bring balance. The over-all goal is not to achieve 10's, but to find a balance. In other words, it would be better to have a range of 4 -6 then have 10's in some areas and 3's in others. If you are scoring high in certain areas you may find that these numbers come down a bit as you work on the low areas. The numbers are not as important as the balance you are trying to seek. After each category you can make notes of goals you would like to set and then journal about them in the next section.

Spiritually

_____ Prayers are not hindered
_____ I often sense God is close to me
_____ I have a healthy fear of God
_____ I am able to feel or sense the pain of others
_____ Spiritual melodies spontaneously come to mind
_____ I am quick to forgive
_____ I have a genuine concern for the welfare of all nationalities
_____ I desire to see miracles that only God can do
_____ I walk in integrity (my values are the same in private as public)

Mentally

_____ I am exercising my mind through regular reading
_____ I give my mind time to rest while I am awake
_____ I have learned to listen and sense things at a deeper level than logic
_____ My imagination is used to bring my creativity to life
_____ My nighttime dreams are healthy
_____ I stay focused when engaged in an assignment

Emotionally

_____ I can cry when appropriate
_____ I have learned to be angry without hurting others
_____ I experience joy and express it to others
_____ It is safe for others to be emotional around me
_____ Expression of the range of emotions is normal
_____ Emotions do not rule my decision-making
_____ I have a language for my emotions (I can tell you what I am feeling using specific words)

Relationally

_____ I have friends at various levels of intimacy
_____ People are important to me because of who they
are, over and above what they can do
_____ I work through conflict rather than avoid it
_____ Serving others gives me pleasure
_____ I can easily allow others to help me
_____ I seek advice and counsel
_____ I can receive loving rebuke or challenge and use it
as a way to grow and mature

Financially

_____ I control my spending
_____ I tithe without complaint
_____ I am a giver
_____ If I borrow money it is to grow investments rather
than just create debt
_____ I always pay my bills on time
_____ My credit report is excellent
_____ Others would say I am a good steward

Physically

_____ I get sufficient rest for my life-style
_____ I am active and or exercise
_____ My blood pressure is in a normal range
_____ My cholesterol is in acceptable ranges
_____ My eating habits are balanced
_____ I feel ready to face whatever comes my way
_____ I value my body by scheduling regular physical
check-ups

113

123

"The future belongs to those who believe in the beauty of dreams."

—Eleanor Roosevelt

3   Inspiring Hope for Your Future

If you have spent a fair amount of time processing your past and balancing your present, it is likely you have captured some hopes, dreams and deep desires that will help you form your life-vision. To successfully inspire your hopes, try to remain open-minded; do not let things like money, time, age, gender or education restrain you. Put aside these factors and ask yourself where you want to be and what you want to be doing five, ten, even twenty-five years down the road. Let your imagination roll; write about relationships you will form, finances you will handle, the impact your vision will have on society, how your family will function and so on. As you continue to dream, don't forget about the fun things like vacations you would like to take, hobbies you want to pursue, things you would like to own and the type of financial package you want to steward.

Your design is very unique and vital to others in this world. It is important to peruse the pages you wrote previously as though you are a detective searching for clues.

- What common themes, thoughts, and likes or dislikes do you see?
- Watch for patterns regarding interests, people, activities, business, social life, etc.

Clues to your future are woven throughout your own pages. It may not look like much right now—or even like you could possibly succeed with the answers you wrote—but don't give up just yet! Often, your wounded areas become part of your success because you learn to provide solutions for the problems that accompany them. Keep in mind that the unfolding of your destiny is like revealing an entire series of mysteries.

Now, take what you've just learned and write a vision or purpose statement. For example, my vision statement is: *To be a friend of God, live a passionate, adventurous life and inspire many others throughout the world to do the same.* People who know me personally could say without a doubt that I "come alive" when helping people through teaching, writing and personal coaching. I enjoy creating materials for my presentations, writing my books and awakening people to life and wholeness. What makes you "come alive?"

This is not a time to panic! The meaning of life is a bit mysterious but discovering some facts about how you see yourself is not. We are trying to discover what motivates you, what makes your heart sing and what you are really passionate about. You will be adjusting this statement as you continue your journey, so don't try to set it in stone immediately. It is interesting that when I ventured into this line of work my vision statement was several paragraphs long. So if you cannot write a quick-to-the-point statement, that's all right. The time will come when you will see more and more who you really are. I don't know if Mother Teresa had an actual written vision statement, but it is obvious as you review her life that she loved people and helped everyone she could, especially children. And for the sake of example, I can summarize Martin Luther King's vision: All people have a life of value and should have equal opportunity.

Lasting change requires emotional involvement and commitment. It is now time to integrate the objectives you stated with undeniable cause. In other words you are so convinced that you have a genuine purpose that painful circumstances will not hold you back. Without this motivation, good intentions do not have power to accomplish anything. We must empower the effectuation of our vision with purpose that facilitates action steps, even when we don't feel like it. Quite frankly, lasting change is something that requires commitment, loyalty and the conscientious decision to be responsible. Yes, these words are strong, but how else will you change? **Have your methods to this point created the results you would really like to be experiencing?**

By using my own life as an example, it would be easy to draw a graph that would demonstrate the times I was not committed, loyal or responsible. The road to good intentions leaves you broken, needy and ready to blame someone else for your condition. Don't get me wrong: life comes at you hard; sometimes life is just not fair! However, there is a greater reality and that is your ability to choose. Today I am offering you an opportunity to step a bit closer to the success you desire. Will you continue the journey thereafter? Only you can decide!

The next step to keeping your future inspired is to set goals with reasonable timelines that you can measure and be held accountable to. You may or may not be a *list* person, but the truth is that when we accomplish goals and can testify about them, we find the strength, courage and desire to press on toward the bigger goals. Having said that, write down the names and contact information of a few close friends who will help and encourage you during the journey. As you share with them it is inevitable that they will become excited with you. Your enthusiasm will inspire them to go after their dreams as well!

Closing comments from the author

As you write the new pages of your life and awaken in your destiny, you will find great satisfaction and a sense of well-being because you will be making the world a better place. There will be challenges that can set you back, but if you review your journal regularly, keeping those previous successes fresh in your memory will rekindle your passion. You are designed for success and you have a vital role to play in attaining it. Remember: change will still happen if you do nothing, but will produce results that may be adverse to your destiny—or you can initiate change that will bring you the results you desire. Dig deep, trust God and believe in yourself!

165

An Invitation

Perhaps you still feel a sense of emptiness deep inside. You may have found a measure of peace, joy and pleasure as you sorted out your past, balanced your present and looked towards your future, but still have an empty place longing to be filled. I once had the same sense of emptiness until I discovered that God really does love me and desires for me to succeed. The need I was experiencing was a separation from the God who created the heavens and earth. I had an idea that this God was real and even went to church. I prayed the prayers, sang the songs and did the church stuff. I also sought the tangible facets of "happiness:" drugs, alcohol, cars, various jobs, money and so on, trying to fill my voids. The world can be a cruel place, but so can the world of dead religion, where there is a form of godliness but no power and no authentic relationships.

God, however, is an amazing being, full of life, power and well-being. His original design for humanity entailed His interactive presence with mankind. No one can fully understand why God's opposing forces (Satan and his legions) were allowed on the earth. I do know that Satan and his evil hosts despise mankind and will do whatever they can to distract them from God their Creator. The subtle temptation that Satan presented to man at the beginning of time was accepted by the first two humans. Hence, sin entered "the world" which entrapped all mankind to be born in sin and in need of salvation from its deadly grip.

Remember, man was created with the intrinsic attribute of freewill and choice. God could not interfere with their (Adam and Eve's) decision. The problem their decision created was that all who followed would be born into a world continually challenged by the temptations of sin.

I believe I have asked all the questions and made all my complaints known to God about the unfairness of this earthly life. When all was said and done and I had exhausted my efforts to find the answers, I decided to seek the truth of my existence, which in part is a restored relationship with Him.

After many losses and failures, including the smashing blow of cancer, I realized that I needed help that man could not provide. I cried out to God and He showed me that simple truth would set me free—not religious activity, not going to church and pretending, not giving my money, not even reading the Bible would set me free. The truth is that the Bible is good for us and instructs us well, but nothing happens when you read mere words without the Spirit of God enlightening you. What I needed was a supernatural encounter with this God who created me. As I mentioned earlier, I had cancer (or should I say cancer had me?). I endured the terrible rounds with chemotherapy, hospital stays and the utter embarrassment of a deteriorating body, eventually finding remission from this evil. Several months later, I had a touch from a Holy God as Randy Clark, the founder of a ministry called Global Awakening, prayed for healing. I will never forget the warmth and the peace that came over me. I left that experience with a total confidence that the cancer had been completely removed from my body because God had healed me. It was during this season of my life when I began to believe that Jesus Christ is the essence of my salvation.

You can choose to awaken yourself to God's kingdom today by accepting Jesus Christ as your Savior. You will discover an ability to see, sense and hear from a new perspective: your personal spirit. After you accept the finished work of Jesus into your heart, the darkness that once separated you from God is removed. Now you are invited to experience a great inheritance, the realm of the Kingdom of God. You were designed to walk on this natural earth as a man or woman, living a supernatural life, alive in your personal spirit and alive to the divine realm of heaven. God did not intend your salvation from sin merely so that you could go to heaven someday; he wants you to beckon heavenly attributes, provision and answers to earth as you learn to relate to Him. He has more than what you need: the plans and purposes He has for you are great. Invite Him to deliver you from the darkness of sin by believing that Jesus Christ is the answer. Take some time and read the Gospels of Matthew, Mark, Luke and John and you will see what I am talking about. I enjoy many translations of the Bible, but if you are new to this I would recommend starting with Eugene Peterson's modern translation called "The Message."

If you want to embark on this experience, simply pray:

"Dear God, I am beginning to see that I am limited in my ability without You. As a matter of fact, I don't even know You. I am lost in my sin, trying to validate my existence. I cannot save myself and need Your help. Today as an act of faith I choose to confess that Jesus Christ is Lord and that He is my answer to a restored relationship with You. Living in this world has been hard and I have chosen to live in sin even though that is not what I really desire. Please forgive me! I accept Jesus Christ as my personal savior and look forward to getting to know You. I am going to need Your help because I don't know how to live in this new state as a born anew Christian. Please fill me with Your Holy Spirit. Please bring safe, trustworthy people into my life that will lead me into Your truth; keep those away who will tempt me into a form of "godliness without power." Open my eyes and ears to see and hear Your truth. Awaken me to the fullness of my personal destiny so that I can positively impact this world. Amen."

Now that you have a personal awareness of God, ask Him to teach you how to pray. Jesus gave us an example in Matthew 6:9-13. *"This then is how you should pray: Our Father in heaven, hallowed be Your name, Your kingdom come, Your will be done on earth as it is in heaven. Give us today our daily bread. Forgive us our debts, as we also have forgiven our debtors. And lead us not into temptation, but deliver us from the evil one."* Take time to read the entire chapter in the New International Version as well as the Message Version of the Bible – it will help change your life.

As you continue your journey you will experience seasons when you may not feel like your relationship with God is real. During these times you can learn a lot from the life of David who was not afraid to share his feelings with God. The book of Psalms which is found in the Old Testament portion of the Bible outlines open and honest confessions of David that are helpful in teaching us to pray, talk to God. You will find that David did not always feel God's presence or feel good about him self. However, he learned he could safely "cast his cares upon the Lord", and He would show care for him. May I encourage you to follow the model of David when you feel down and out, lost or confused! Share your deepest feelings and thoughts with God and He will care for you. Jesus said, "Blessed are those who mourn, for they shall be comforted." (Matthew 5:4)

I too, along with David have learned that when I truly share my heart with God concerning how I feel, I am less likely to hurt others when I am feeling distressed or angry. Matthew 5:9 (Message) gives us and important truth: "You're blessed when you can show people how to cooperate instead of compete or fight. That's when you discover who you really are, and your place in God's family."

We also need to consider that sin can still cause problems in our lives after our salvation experience. God provided an answer for this in I John 1:9, "If we confess our sins, He is faithful and just and will forgive us our sins and purify us from all unrighteousness." Therefore you can come into alignment with the protection of heaven and be free from false guilt and condemnation by seeking forgiveness, receiving forgiveness and giving forgiveness. Remember, hurting people, hurt people; which means you will need to learn the essence of forgiveness in daily life.

If you prayed the prayer, previously outlined, and would like more information send us an email at info@destinyui.com or call (717) 627-0480.

203

We would also enjoy hearing your testimonies concerning how your destiny and purpose became a greater reality to you as you went through this journaling process. If we are able to use your testimony as an affirmation to the effectiveness of this journal we will send you a $25.00 gift certificate to use in our online store.

Thank you for the opportunity to share with you!
Respectfully,
Rob Stoppard

About the Artist, Nancy Stawitz

Nancy has an intrinsic love of both art and science. She received an associates degree in commercial art from Antonelli Institute of Art and Photography in 1987, and joined The Pfaltzgraff Company for 15 years designing dinnerware and stainless steel flatware.

She received a Certificate of Merit in Ornamental Horticulture from Longwood Gardens in 2000 and enjoyed designing many gardens.

With a love for travel and adventure, Nancy has been to Europe and the Middle East. One of the most inspirational trips was to Japan in 1999, where she immersed herself in Japanese gardens and culture. During the summer of 2003, she spent six weeks in Barcelona, Spain, taking in all the art and architecture the city had to offer.

In 2002, Nancy left Pfaltzgraff to go out on her own. She worked as a freelance designer for four years and found joy in painting her own silk painting, watercolors and acrylics.

In 2005, she felt drawn to explore the Adirondack region of Lake George, NY. Many unusual coincidences and adventures led to her discovery of a strong heart desire to help people relax and find restoration in nature.

Nancy is currently attending the Baltimore School of Massage, York Campus. Upon her graduation she desires to create a business that will incorporate all of the paths that have led her to where she is today.

Her life is rooted in spirituality. It is the center and spring from which everything else flows. She sees life as an adventure to be lived at one with the Creator, and this is what makes her feel alive.

Nancy lives in New Cumberland, PA, with Kiwi, a Gold-Capped Conure; Kayenta, a dingo (dog); and cats, Domino and Judah.

You can contact Nancy at (717) 770-0569 or nancy.stawitz@verizon.net

About the Author, Rob Stoppard

Rob Stoppard has seen what life is like without a clear destiny and purpose. Cancer was the diagnosis—the prognosis grim. Yet, Rob received healing—and a year later, in 1997, Rob began to realize a vision for helping individuals discover wholeness and vision for their lives. The whole course of his life was shifted from an 18-year career in construction to developing his gifts in counseling, teaching, life-coaching, team building and leadership development. While making the shift in focus, Rob spent eight years leading his own building business, where he learned many things not to do! Consequently, he discovered many of the pitfalls that plague business owners and organizational leaders.

Risk to Change...

For more than eight years, Rob has been dedicated to helping individuals and organizations discover vision for life, personal wholeness, and the fullness of prosperity. During this season he founded Breath of Life Ministries in Ephrata, Pennsylvania, and served as the Director for five years. Rob also served as the Northeast Regional Director for Elijah House, an international counseling and training organization. Rob spent thousands of hours in personal counsel and coaching sessions, facilitated many training events and has coached numerous leaders in church organizations and businesses in vision development, team building and personal growth.

Personally Speaking...

Rob loves to learn and continues to spend serious amounts of time developing his gifts in leadership development, business consultation, life-coaching and vision development. Rob and his beautifully energetic wife, Ann, live in Lititz, Pennsylvania. They have two sons and a beautiful daughter-in-law: Joshua and his wife Jessica and Matthew.

New Way...

The development of *Destiny Unlimited International* has been a very natural extension, as Rob has a keen insight into relational concerns and strengths which may either distract from or enhance the ability to prosper and develop a personal or corporate vision. A key to success is discovering what makes your heart "sing"—in other words, what you are really passionate about. Once that discovery is made, we can help you build a more meaningful and fulfilling life founded on the truth of your personal or corporate destiny.

Destiny Unlimited International

We have found the journey of a prosperous life requires *risk, relationships with right values*. Many never realize their dreams because they believe the things they enjoy thinking about or doing could never become a profitable career. Rob is gifted to discover what is not being said and where there are hidden barriers to growth and prosperity.

We help individuals and organizations through:

Personal growth seminars and workshops
- Alive in Your Destiny
- Encounters with Freedom
- The Freedom and Life Series

Personal life coaching
Many people need that little inspirational push to keep them on target as they walk out their unique personal journey of life. A good coach provides encouragement to set goals and stay on course according to your own desires and dreams.

Life coach training
We are developing the Life Coach Exchange which offers special training from our unique experiences helping people of diverse backgrounds and needs. We provide simple solutions through practical worksheets and coaching principles that can be learned by anyone with a heart for people.

Vision development
- Enlarge personal life vision/purpose
- Cultivate marriage vision/purpose
- Develop family vision/purpose

People, marriages, families without vision lose out in life. People with purpose accomplish their hopes and dreams. We help individuals, couples and families set a course to a future that is custom-designed for their unique situations.

Contact us at
Destiny Unlimited International
406 W. Lexington Rd. Lititz, PA 17543
(717) 627-0480   www.destinyui.com

Destiny Unlimited International offers insights for Business

All of our principles are also very effective for businesses and organizations. Many business leaders work far too hard and focus on the inconsequential—simply due to a lack of vision and an inability to integrate personal destiny with the corporate vision. *Destiny Unlimited International* can help you pinpoint personal and corporate vision and create meaningful goals to fulfillment through:

Enlarging company vision, mission and core-values
Vision is an incredible force when carefully infused with strategy for development and shared by people who are alive in their personal destiny.

Strengthening leadership through personal growth
Many leaders are over-stressed and tired. Practical adjustments in everyday life that are personal and profitable inspire strength for decision-making and courage to lead the changes necessary to excel in your goals.

Developing life-giving teams
Trust, open and honest communication, commitment and accountability lead to corporate results. Our simple approach removes the false harmony that is a result of a lack of trust. The end result inspires creativity, provides solutions and increases profits.

Mediation—resolving relational problems
Profits are directly impacted by the harmony of relationships. A relational coach provides an atmosphere for open and honest communication that ends in a win–win position for all concerned

Flippen Personal Profile Assessment
A precise and predictive online assessment that is easy to use. It accurately creates a custom action plan with target-specific, action-oriented coaching statements for lasting personal growth.

Contact us at
Destiny Unlimited International
406 W. Lexington Rd. Lititz, PA 17543
(717) 627-0480   www.destinyui.com